God's Story
to the Nations

In the Beginning

God's Story
to the Nations:
In the Beginning

Jody Stelly

God's Story to the Nations: In the Beginning
Copyright © 2023 by Jody Stelly

Illustrated by Amanda Ravensdale
Published by Lucid Books in Houston, TX
www.LucidBooks.com

Scripture quotations marked (ESV) are taken from the ESV® Bible (The Holy Bible, English Standard Version®), copyright © 2001 by Crossway, a publishing ministry of Good News Publishers. Used by permission. All rights reserved.

Scripture quotations marked (NIV) are taken from the Holy Bible, New International Version®, NIV®. Copyright ©1973, 1978, 1984, 2011 by Biblica, Inc.™ Used by permission of Zondervan. All rights reserved worldwide. www.zondervan.com The "NIV" and "New International Version" are trademarks registered in the United States Patent and Trademark Office by Biblica, Inc.™

Scripture quotations marked (NLT) are taken from the Holy Bible, New Living Translation, copyright ©1996, 2004, 2015 by Tyndale House Foundation. Used by permission of Tyndale House Publishers, Carol Stream, Illinois 60188. All rights reserved.

All rights reserved. No part of this publication may be reproduced, stored in a retrieval system, or transmitted in any form by any means, electronic, mechanical, photocopy, recording, or otherwise, without the prior permission of the publisher, except as provided for by USA copyright law.

ISBN: 978-1-63296-592-9 Paperback
ISBN: 978-1-63296-593-6 Hardback
eISBN: 978-1-63296-594-3

Special Sales: Lucid Books titles are available in special quantity discounts. Custom imprinting or excerpting can also be done to fit special needs. Contact Lucid Books at Info@LucidBooks.com

Table of Contents

Preface	iii
Introduction	1
The Creator of All Things – GENESIS 1	3
Story	4
Commentary	8
God Creates Humanity in His Image – GENESIS 2	11
Story	12
Commentary	16
The Fall – GENESIS 3	19
Story	20
Commentary	24
The First Family – GENESIS 4	27
Story	28
Commentary	32
The Flood – GENESIS 6–9	35
Story	36
Commentary	40
The Tower of Babel – GENESIS 11	43
Story	44
Commentary	48
Afterword	51
Notes	53

Preface

How beautiful are the feet of messengers who bring good news!
—Romans 10:15 NLT

This storying initiative was born out of God's leading, years of missiological research, and the necessity to make God's story available to Indigenous tribal peoples who do not have the ability to read. This project was designed, developed, and written as an Audio Bible Storying project to make biblical stories accessible to those plagued by illiteracy in the Majority World. Many peoples in the world today are part of oral cultures where the primary means of communicating and passing along their heritage and history is done verbally. Oral Bible Storying has proven effective in many contexts among different people groups. This method allows those who cannot read to hear God's story in a familiar way, and it also equips and trains believers to be good storytellers and share the good news of Jesus with others.

As the audio portion of the project continues to move forward and more of God's story is made available to Indigenous peoples, it is exciting to put these Bible stories and the accompanying commentaries into print along with illustrations to be shared with others.

And this gospel of the kingdom will be preached in the whole world as a testimony to all nations, and then the end will come.
—Matthew 24:14 NIV

Introduction

This book contains the beginning of God's story in the Book of Genesis, chapters 1 to 11. This will be an exciting journey through biblical history starting with the Creation and ending with the dispersal of the peoples from the Tower of Babel. Each narrative tells the truth of God's Word contained in the Book of Genesis and is accompanied by a commentary to help shed light on what is occurring and to help the reader see the significance of each part of God's story.

Each narrative is delightfully illustrated to creatively express the beauty and meaningfulness of the message given to us by the Lord. Jesus is our Creator and has revealed His great love, mercy, and grace for us throughout biblical history! When we share God's story, He is faithful to see it through and accomplish all He intends in the world today. These very stories are proving fruitful among different people groups in India as local missionaries are trained in storytelling and equipped with audio versions in local dialects. It is a blessing to make them available in this format, and it is exciting to think of how the Lord will use them.

These Bible stories are designed to be short and fairly easy to remember. It is my hope that the Lord will use them to produce much lasting fruit among the nations through this printed and illustrated format.

Let's embark on this journey as we explore the beginning of God's story.

The Creator of All Things
GENESIS 1

The Creator of All Things

GENESIS 1

STORY

In the beginning, Almighty God created all things out of nothing. In six days, He created the heavens and the earth; God spoke all things into existence. On Day 1, "God said, 'Let there be light,' and there was light. God saw that the light was good, and he separated the light from the darkness. God called the light 'day' and the darkness 'night.'"[1]

On Day 2, God created the atmosphere that made the earth sustainable for life. He separated the waters into the water above and waters below, creating an expanse between them which He called "sky."

On Day 3, God created the oceans and made dry land appear to grow rich vegetation producing fruit and seed. God sprouted the land with trees, shrubs, grasses, and fungi that would provide food for and sustain life.

On Day 4, God created the cosmos with countless stars and galaxies. He said these lights in the heavens would be for signs of the seasons and to mark days and years. He created the sun to rule the day and the moon to rule the night, and both were precisely positioned to sustain life on earth.

On Day 5, God created all aquatic and aerial organisms. He filled the waters of the earth with abundant life such as fish, whales, and crustaceans. He filled the skies with a rich diversity of birds, bats, and waterfowl.

On Day 6, God created all terrestrial organisms, both wildlife and livestock, that roamed the dry land. He filled the ecosystems of the land with mammals, reptiles, and insects. God saw all that he had created. "And God saw that it was good."[2]

"Then God said, 'Let us make man in our image, after our likeness. And let them have dominion over'"[3] all the earth and its ecosystems. So, God created humanity in His image–He created them male and female. "And God blessed them. And God said to them, 'Be fruitful and multiply and fill the earth.'"[4] Then "God saw all that He had made, and it was very good."[5]

The Creator of All Things

GENESIS 1

COMMENTARY

Genesis 1 is the very beginning of God's story, and it is the first recorded history given to us by God in the biblical timeline. The power and majesty of God's spoken word is revealed as He creates all things. Not only do we learn that He is the Creator of all things, but we see that God is a god of the details. Our Creator has been and still is concerned about the very details and timing of our lives. God is the masterful engineer who created precision and purpose into all His creation. From the precise tilt of the earth on its axis to the positions and distances of the sun and moon, God's design was not by chance. The world was created to work in unity to support life in God's new world. He designed it to be a wonderful world filled with rich biodiversity–a very good world teaming with beautiful wildlife, fish, livestock, vegetation, and flora–all declaring the Glory of God and giving us a picture of who He is.

God so cared about the details that He created you and me in His image, and He cares intimately about each of us as His child. It is comforting to know that the Creator of all things knows each of us by name and cares about us each and every day. Go outside today and take notice of the Creator's handiwork—appreciate the rays of sunlight on your face; the clouds in the expanse of the sky; the trees, grass, flowers, and crops; the birds chirping and flying through the air; and the moon and stars of the night—all declaring the wonders of His hand. Above all, take comfort that God loves you and has cared about you since the beginning.

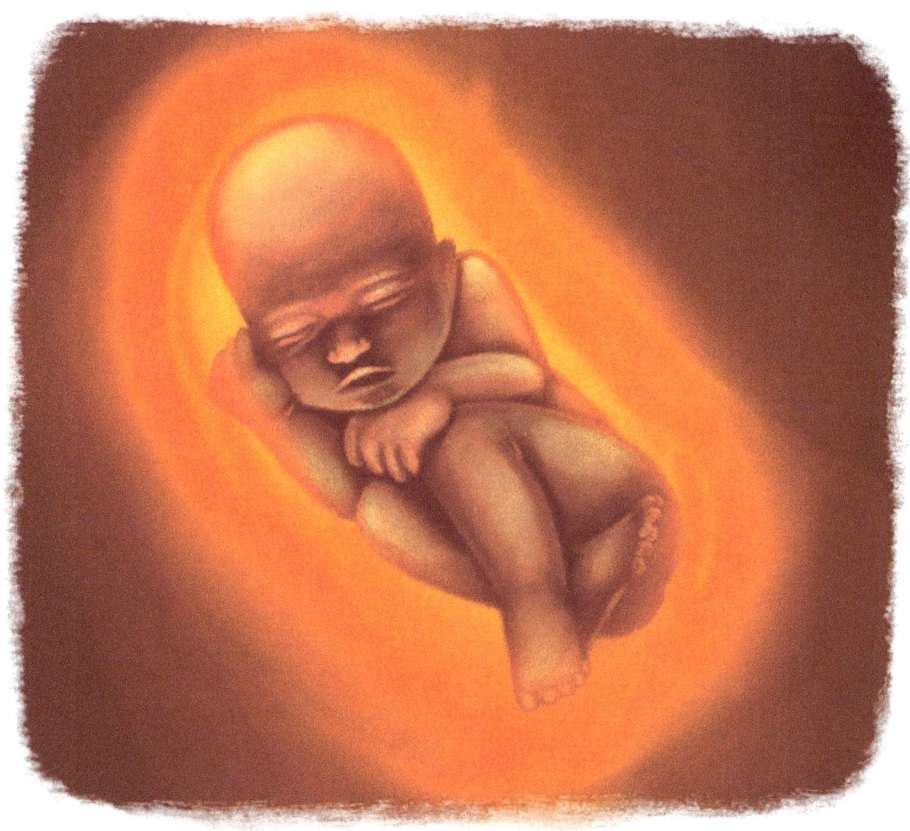

God Creates Humanity in His Image
GENESIS 2

God Creates Humanity in His Image

GENESIS 2

STORY

God created all things in six days and after His work was done, He rested. God rested on the seventh day, and He "blessed the seventh day and made it holy."[6] God's very good creation was without blemish and just as He intended. God had created humanity in His image. He formed the first man, Adam, "from the dust of the ground and breathed"[7] life into his nostrils. God prepared a garden for Adam that contained every tree that was "pleasing to the eye and good for food."[8]

This garden contained two special trees–the tree of life and the tree of the knowledge of good and evil. God placed Adam in the Garden of Eden to work and keep it. The Lord God commanded Adam that he could eat from every tree in the garden except one–the tree of the knowledge of good and evil. But if Adam ate from that tree, he would surely die.

As Adam worked and kept the garden, God declared that it was not good for man to be alone and planned to give him a helper. Now God brought every created beast of the field and bird of the heavens to Adam "to see what he would call them. And whatever the man called every living creature, that was its name."⁹ Adam named all the living creatures, but for Adam there was still no helper to be found.

So, the Lord God placed Adam in a deep sleep and took one of his ribs. From Adam's rib, God created the first woman and brought her to him. When Adam saw the woman, he was blessed by God's provision, and he named her Eve. Eve was the helper God intended so that Adam would not be alone. They were the world's first couple and God instructed that a man shall leave his parents "and hold fast to his wife, and they shall become one flesh"¹⁰ in the covenant of marriage. The new couple were together enjoying communion with God in the Garden of Eden. Adam and Eve "were both naked and were not ashamed"¹¹ as they cared for God's very good creation.

God Creates Humanity in His Image

GENESIS 2

COMMENTARY

Genesis 2 opens with God blessing and making the seventh day holy. After God had spoken His very good creation into existence in six days, He rested on the seventh day. This is an important example set for us–that we should take a day of rest after six days of work. This day of rest would later be called the Sabbath, which was the seventh day and set aside for God's people to worship and abstain from work. If the Creator of all things found it important to rest, it is probably important that we too observe a day of rest from work and worship the Lord God.

In Genesis 2, God gives more details about creating humanity in His image on Day 6. God created Adam from the earth, placed him in the Garden of Eden, and gave him dominion or control over creation. Adam even had the privilege of naming all the living creatures that God created. God knew from the very beginning that Adam needed a helper, so He created Eve from Adam's rib.

From the very beginning, God shows us His design for marriage, family, and the oneness intended between a husband and his wife. The first couple were together in the Garden of Eden, and there was no blemish on God's very good creation. God tells us that Adam and Eve were naked in the garden and were not ashamed. This is an indication that they were innocent—without sin or guilt, and thus had no shame. Because they were righteous, Adam and Eve enjoyed fellowship and walked with God in the garden.

The Fall

GENESIS 3

The Fall

GENESIS 3

STORY

As Adam and Eve were tending and caring for God's creation in the Garden of Eden, the Enemy came in the form of a serpent with the intention of bringing doubt and deception. One day when Eve was foraging in the garden, the serpent came to her and began to ask questions. Satan asked, "Did God really say, 'You must not eat from any tree in the garden'?"[12] Eve shared God's instruction about the tree of the knowledge of good and evil, but the serpent told half-truths in deception. He said, "You will not surely die!"[13] In that moment of temptation, Eve took fruit from the tree, ate, and gave some to Adam who also ate the forbidden fruit.

Then, "their eyes were opened,"[14] and Adam and Eve knew they were naked. "So they sewed fig leaves together to cover themselves,"[15] for they were ashamed. Then they heard the Lord walking in the garden and hid themselves among the trees. The Lord called out to Adam, and he answered from his hiding place saying, "I heard you walking in the garden, so I hid. I was afraid because I am naked."[16] God knew what they had done, and He asked Adam if he had disobeyed and eaten from the tree he was commanded not to.

Adam immediately blamed his wife: "The woman whom you gave to be with me, she gave me fruit of the tree, and I ate."[17] Eve immediately blamed the serpent saying, "The serpent deceived me, and I ate."[18] The Lord God was not pleased, and He cursed the serpent, promising that the offspring of the woman would crush the serpent's head with his heel. God clearly told Adam and Eve that there would be serious consequences for their disobedience. Their unrighteousness brought sin, pain, and death into God's very good creation.

The first couple could no longer stay in the garden and be in the presence of the Lord. Mankind would have to labor and work the cursed ground for provision because of their actions until the day they died and returned to the dust. So, God sent Adam and Eve out of the garden to work the ground from which Adam had been made. But before they left, God made them garments from animal skins and clothed them.

The Fall

GENESIS 3

COMMENTARY

Genesis 3 marks a very significant period in biblical history known as the Fall. The moment of deception and disobedience that occurred in the garden would forever change the course of history. At the Fall, Adam and Eve's disobedience corrupted God's very good creation and ushered in the sin, death, pain, and suffering that plagues the world till this very day. With the Fall, sinful man could no longer dwell in the presence of the Lord. Not only were Adam and Eve sent away from the garden and God's presence, but all their offspring would also be born unrighteous and incapable of communion with a Holy God.

The Fall also impacted the rest of God's creation as the geological and ecological balance was corrupted, leading to natural disasters, predator-prey dynamics, and even genetic impacts that cause disease. When sin entered God's very good creation, its perfect balance and unity were corrupted. But the good news is that God had a plan for redemption from the very beginning. When God promised that Eve's offspring would crush the serpent's head, that was the first recorded redemptive promise of God. God was promising that His Son Jesus (who would come through Eve's offspring) would undo the damage that the serpent caused at the tree of the knowledge of good and evil. Jesus would pay the wages of sin, so that humanity could be right before God again. Just as God showed His love and mercy to Adam and Eve by clothing them before sending them out of the garden, the Lord shows His love and mercy to all of us by sending Jesus as our Savior and Redeemer.

The First Family
GENESIS 4

The First Family

GENESIS 4

STORY

Adam and Eve started their life outside the Garden of Eden, and they had two sons: Cain and Abel. Cain was a farmer who worked the ground, and Abel was a shepherd who tended sheep.

During a harvest season, the brothers each prepared an offering for the Lord God. Cain brought "an offering of the fruit of the ground, and Abel also brought of the firstborn of his flock and of their fat portions"[19] to the Lord. The Lord God was pleased with Abel's offering but had no regard for Cain's offering. Because of this, Cain became very angry. "The Lord said to Cain, 'Why are you angry, and why has your face fallen? If you do well, will you not be accepted? And if you do not do well, sin is crouching at the door. Its desire is contrary to you, but you must rule over it.'"[20]

One day when they were out "in the field, Cain rose up against his brother Abel and killed him. Then the Lord said to Cain, 'Where is Abel your brother?'"[21] Cain lied to God and said, "'I do not know; am I my brother's keeper?' And the Lord said, 'What have you done? The voice of your brother's blood is crying out to me from the ground.'"[22]

God cursed Cain for what he had done. The ground would no longer bear fruit for him, and Cain became a fugitive, destined to wander the earth. "Then Cain went away from the presence of the Lord and settled in the land of Nod, East of Eden."[23]

After Abel's death and Cain's departure, Adam and Eve were alone again. They would have another son appointed for them by God. They named him Seth. As the human population grew from the first family, the people began to call upon the name of the Lord.

The First Family

GENESIS 4

COMMENTARY

Genesis 4 continues God's story by sharing about the first family of the world. During creation week, God created Adam and Eve with His own hands and commanded them to be fruitful and multiply. Cain and Abel were the first human-born individuals; God used them to give us a picture of family. As with many families today, we see that the first family also had its troubles and problems because of sin that was introduced into His very good creation at the Fall.

In Genesis 4, we see the first recorded acts of worship in Scripture as Cain and Abel present offerings to the Lord God. God was pleased with Abel because he gave the first of what he had to the Lord along with fat portions, which were considered the best. Although Cain brought an offering from his crops, the Lord had no regard for Cain's offering. While there is limited detail, the Lord knows the posture of our hearts and our motives as we worship. The Lord's disregard for Cain's offering angered Cain very much. Through Cain, God warns us that if we do well, we will be accepted, but if we do not do well, "sin is crouching at the door."[24] God tells us clearly that sin is contrary to who He created us to be and that we must rule over it.

One day while they were out in the field, "Cain rose up against his brother Abel and killed him."[25] Cain's sinfulness and desire for vengeance got the best of him. Cain was so angry because his offering was not regarded by the Lord, that he became jealous of his brother Abel. Likewise, our sinfulness has consequences, and we are all accountable before God. God cursed Cain because of what he had done and caused him to wander the earth, away from His presence. After Abel's death and Cain's departure, Adam and Eve were blessed with another son whom they named Seth. Seth was God's provision through whom He continued His story, eventually sending His Son, Jesus.

The Flood

GENESIS 6-9

The Flood
GENESIS 6-9

STORY

As the human population of the earth continued to increase, people began to grow more and more wicked. This was around 1,550 years after the Creation, and "the Lord saw that every intention of the thoughts of [man's] heart was only evil."[26] This grieved God, and He "regretted that he had made man on the earth."[27]

But there was a man named Noah who found favor with the Lord. Noah was a righteous man who walked with God. God explained to Noah that He planned to destroy all things of the earth because of the corruption and violence. God gave Noah very specific instructions. God told Noah to build an ark of gopher wood measuring 510 feet long and over 50 feet tall comprised of 3 levels. The ark would protect Noah, his family, and all the living creatures onboard from the global flood that God would send to wipe the earth clean. For over one hundred years, Noah warned the people about the coming flood as he constructed the ark with the help of his three sons. When the time came, God sent two of every created kind (male and female) into the ark. All those within the ark would be saved. Many people of his day made fun of Noah as he told them of the judgment to come—even as Noah's family boarded the ark, and God shut the door.

As promised, God ripped open the great fountains of the deep, "and rain fell upon the earth forty days and forty nights."[28] The flood waters covered the earth above the tallest mountains and persisted for over a year. This global catastrophe involved earthquakes, volcanic eruptions, tsunamis, massive erosion, and deposition of sediment; it completely changed the face of the earth. As promised, God destroyed all except those protected by the ark.

Once the water receded, God told Noah and his family to go out from the ark, to be fruitful and multiply, and to fill the earth. The Lord promised never to destroy the earth with a flood again and marked His promise by placing a rainbow in the sky.

The Flood
GENESIS 6-9

COMMENTARY

Genesis 6 to 9 gives us an account of the judgment that God brought upon the earth because of humanity's wickedness. Scripture tells us that things were so bad that God regretted creating man and that their sin grieved the heart of the Lord. God sent a global flood to destroy everything that was on the earth. This global catastrophe was more than just rain falling; it consisted of massive geologic events such as earthquakes, volcanic eruptions, and tsunamis that rapidly impacted the biosphere and changed the face of the earth forever. The global flood is the historical event that deposited massive layers of sediment that span the earth containing fossils formed from the remains of the created kinds destroyed by God. The only aerial and terrestrial creatures that survived the flood were those protected by the ark that Noah faithfully built.

By God's mercy and grace, He provided a way for Noah and his family along with a pair (male and female) of every created kind to be saved. Those saved on the ark would be commanded to multiply and fill the earth. They would be the ones through whom God's story would continue. Noah's family are the ancestors to all modern-day human beings on earth. God promised not to destroy the earth by water again and marked His promise with a rainbow.

However, there is coming a second judgment, and that one will be by fire (2 Peter 3:7). And just as God provided a way of salvation during the global flood in the form of an ark, the Lord has provided a way of salvation from the judgment to come. "For God so loved the world" [even after the disobedience and wickedness of man] "that he gave his only son,"[29] Jesus. Jesus is our hope and salvation; He makes a way for us to live just as the ark provided during Noah's day. The ark only provided physical protection, but the Lord Jesus provides salvation and eternal life to all who profess with their mouths that He is Lord and believe in their hearts that God raised Him from the dead (Romans 10:9).

The Tower of Babel

GENESIS 11

The Tower of Babel

GENESIS 11

STORY

After the global flood, the nations descended from Noah through his three sons—Shem, Ham, and Japheth. About 100 years after the flood, the earth's population had only one language, and they settled on "a plain in the land of Shinar."[30] They began to develop and hone their craftsmanship of making bricks and mortar. With these skills, they decided to build a city for themselves and a tower that would stretch toward the heavens. The people desired to make a name for themselves and to avoid being dispersed over the face of the earth. This was contrary to what the Lord had commanded when Noah exited the ark: God had commanded them to multiply and fill the earth.

"The Lord came down to see the city and the tower the people were building."[31] He was not pleased with what He observed. Instead of filling the earth, the people had decided to stay together and make a name for themselves. To thwart their efforts, the Lord God confused their language. The people could no longer communicate, so they stopped building the city and were dispersed over the face of the whole earth. The unfinished city "was called Babel—because there the Lord confused the language of the whole world."[32] God's purpose and plan for repopulating the earth was once again on track, and it would be through the lineage of Noah's son Shem that God would call a man named Abram to continue His story.

The Tower of Babel

GENESIS 11

COMMENTARY

Genesis 11 occurs only about 100 years after the global flood, and it illustrates that it doesn't take long for people to forget all that God has done for them in the past. This is a clear demonstration of man's desire for independence and self-sufficiency apart from God. The people became so confident in their own abilities that they did not look to God for provision. Their pride led them to desire a great name for themselves instead of dispersing over the earth as God had commanded. The Lord God was not pleased with the people's unified, self-confidence and their disobedience and pride. God confused their language, and the people were dispersed throughout the earth as the Lord intended. Because of God's love, mercy, and grace, He continues to have an interest in His creation, and this dispersal facilitated the development of all nations consisting of different cultures and peoples. It ultimately prepared the way for Abram (a descendant of Noah's son Shem) to be called by God and to be the pathway through which the whole world would be blessed.

The Tower of Babel shows us a historical picture of man's disobedience toward God combined with our own sinfulness of pride and self-reliance. Throughout history, mankind has struggled with a desire to be overly independent, relying on their own skills, knowledge, and self-sufficiency.

We must always remember what God has done for us and never lose focus of our reliance on Him and Him alone. God's provision is infinitely rich, and He uniquely gifts each of us to accomplish His purposes. We must continually strive to be in the Lord's will and to steer clear of our own prideful endeavors that will lead us astray.

Afterword

I pray that you have enjoyed this journey through the opening of God's story. It is imperative that we appeal to the truth of the Creator and allow His Creation to bear witness (Romans 1:20). The stories in this book were designed and written with that very principle in mind. In Majority World contexts today, Christianity is viewed primarily as a foreign religion (specifically as Western in most contexts). But the opening chapters of Scripture, Genesis 1 to 11, show us a commonalty that we all share as human beings.

At the beginning of God's story, we gain insight about creation—not only that there is a Creator but that He loves us and made us His prized possession created in His very image! God shows us His design for gender, marriage, and family as well as ethnic and cultural diversity. From my experience, even the most remote tribal people, never having been exposed to the gospel, have an inherent knowledge of a Supreme Being who created all things that they rely on for existence. Sharing the beginning of God's story becomes a bridge of mutual respect and relationship that leads to deeper conversations about the gospel and the truth about Jesus.

As a Christian educator, I am convinced that those of us privileged to live in developed nations with wonderful educational systems need the truth of Genesis 1 to 11 now more than ever. Our society is plagued with secular theories that stand in stark contrast to the truth of God's Word. If we don't truly understand the beginning of God's story, secular theories and educational influences will likely lead us to undermine the truth of Genesis and fall victim to relativism, which has serious theological implications. If we can't trust the opening pages of Scripture, that calls into question the inerrant and infallible nature of the whole Bible. God has given us His story, which is to be used "for teaching, rebuking, correcting, and training in righteousness."[33]

We can trust the whole Word of God from Genesis 1:1 to Revelation 22:21 and allow it to illuminate our paths as we walk with Jesus. The Lord Jesus has also called us to share His story with the nations and train others to do the same (Matthew 28:19–20). My hope is that these stories will not only touch your life but that you will also use them for Kingdom purposes as you recall what God has done from the very beginning and share that truth with others.

If you have enjoyed this book and value the Kingdom purpose behind it, please consider supporting future initiatives as more of God's Story is being prepared for storytelling and translated into Indigenous languages. We are also equipping additional storytellers to share within their various contexts. You can learn more and donate if you feel so led at www.gopartnerequip.org.

About The Author

Dr. Jody Stelly is a retired Marine Officer turned missiologist and Christian educator. His educational background is in both science (BS, Renewable Natural Resources Ecology & Management; MS, Environmental Policy & Management) and ministry (MA, Christian Ministry with a concentration in Creation Apologetics; Doctor of Intercultural Studies).

Along with teaching at the secondary and undergraduate levels, Dr. Stelly has pastored in a local church and partnered in church-planting and discipleship efforts among Indigenous peoples in India. He currently resides with his family in East Asia as they walk out the calling that the Lord has given them among the nations.

Notes

[1] Gen. 1:3–5 NIV
[2] Gen. 1:25 ESV
[3] Gen. 1:26 ESV
[4] Gen. 1:28 ESV
[5] Gen. 1:31 ESV
[6] Gen. 2:3 ESV
[7] Gen. 2:7 ESV
[8] Gen. 2:9 NIV
[9] Gen. 2:19 ESV
[10] Gen. 2:24 ESV
[11] Gen. 2:25 ESV
[12] Gen. 3:1 NIV
[13] Gen. 3:4 ESV
[14] Gen. 3:7 NLT
[15] Gen. 3:7 NLT
[16] Gen. 3:10 NLT
[17] Gen. 3:12 ESV
[18] Gen. 3:13 ESV
[19] Gen. 4:3–4 ESV
[20] Gen. 4:6–7 ESV
[21] Gen. 4:8–9 ESV
[22] Gen. 4:9–10 ESV
[23] Gen. 4:16 ESV
[24] Gen. 4:7 ESV
[25] Gen. 4:8 ESV
[26] Gen. 6:5 ESV
[27] Gen. 6:6 ESV
[28] Gen. 7:12 ESV
[29] Gen. 3:16 ESV
[30] Gen. 11:2 ESV
[31] Gen. 11:5 NIV
[32] Gen. 11:9 NIV
[33] Tim. 3:16 NIV